Stable Summits

Mindful Leadership in Turbulent Times

Table of Contents

Chapter 1. Introduction

Navigating the rough waters of leadership during uncertain times can feel like a daunting task. But fear not, our Special Report, "Stable Summits: Mindful Leadership in Turbulent Times" is here to be your compass. This empowering and insightful guide dispels the fog surrounding leadership challenges, shining a light on adaptive, mindful strategies. It seeks to embolden leaders from all sectors to embrace change, displaying how to pilot their organizations towards success even amidst daunting storms of adversity. Captivating case studies, expert insights, and action-oriented tips await – a treasure trove of wisdom that's sure to invigorate your leadership journey. Don't let uncertainty stop your ascent. It's time to conquer those stable summits!

Chapter 2. The Bedrock of Resilience: Understanding Mindful Leadership

Mindfulness has been creating waves not only in personal wellbeing, but in the corporate world as well, which is beginning to recognize mindfulness as a tool not just for stress management, but for enhancing leadership acumen as well. Mindful leadership stems from the application of mindfulness principles in a leadership context. It means being fully present, aware of your own feelings and those of others, and remaining focused on the task at hand. It is about keeping a clear, open mindset, even under turbulent conditions.

2.1. Establishing the Foundation: What is Mindful Leadership?

Mindful leadership is the effective implementation of mindfulness techniques within a leadership framework. It refers to leaders who cultivate focus, clarity, creativity, and compassion in the service of others. Mindful leaders lead with an awareness of their environment and the people within it, responding rather than reacting to challenges that arise.

An integral part of mindful leadership is developing emotional intelligence, often known as EQ, which consists of self-awareness, self-management, social awareness, and relationship management. When leaders step out of autopilot mode and engage their EQ, they become more sensitive to the needs of their employees, fostering better relationships and, in turn, a stronger, more resilient organization.

2.2. The Power of Being Present: Focusing on the Here and Now

A key attribute of mindful leadership is being attentive to the existing moment, or "being present". This may sound simple, but in our fast-paced digital world, our attention is continually pulled in multiple directions. Leaders often find themselves multitasking, with their mind always on the next thing, rather than fully focusing on the present task or conversation.

Mindful leaders cultivate a practice of grounding themselves in the present, creating space between their actions and reactions. This allows them to make more informed, considered decisions that can mitigate risk and lead to better outcomes.

Developing mindfulness, and thereby being present, can be achieved through a variety of techniques. Simple breathing exercises, meditation, yoga, and tapping into the five senses are some methods leaders can use to better connect with the present moment.

2.3. Leading with Compassion: The Human Element in Leadership

Compassion is not often a term associated with leadership – but it should be. Compassionate leadership is a key element of mindfulness. It involves considering the feelings and experiences of employees and responding with empathy and understanding.

The importance of empathy in leadership cannot be overstated. It allows leaders to connect on a deeper level with those they lead. A compassionate leader is more likely to build trust, foster open communication, and encourage a supportive workplace culture where employees feel valued. This helps reduce stress, boost morale, and ultimately, enhances productivity.

2.4. Cultivating an Open Mind: Embracing Versatility and Adaptability

Mindful leaders understand that change is the only constant, and they approach it with an open and flexible mindset. They embrace challenges as opportunities for growing and learning. In adverse situations, instead of panicking or adopting a defensive approach, diversity of thought allows them to explore multiple angles and possibilities.

Adapting to change also involves having an outward mindset, considering the bigger picture and external perspectives. It's about understanding that everyone has a unique journey and recognizing the importance of diverse perspectives in finding novel solutions to complex problems.

2.5. Building Resilient Teams: Empowerment Through Mindful Leadership

It is the role of a mindful leader not just to exhibit these qualities themselves, but to train and perpetuate them throughout their team or organization. Mindful leaders produce more resilient teams by modeling mindful behavior and encouraging their members to do the same. They foster an atmosphere of mutual respect, where team members are tuned to their responsibilities, the present moment, and to each other.

When stress levels peak, mindful teams can remain calm, composed, and effective. They stay anchored in their purpose and maintain their focus on long-term goals, rather than getting swept along by momentary setbacks or failures. Such empowered teams become the vessels of resilience that can skillfully navigate uncertain terrains.

In an era when uncertainty is the new normal, mindful leadership provides the compass for leaders to guide their teams amidst the chaos. It is the cornerstone for building a resilient organization that can not only survive, but thrive in the face of adversity.

Chapter 3. Navigating Uncertainty: Strategies for Leading Through Turbulence

Uncertainty is akin to being in a dense fog, where the path ahead is obscured, and your vision is impaired. It can be quite disorienting, especially when you are in a leadership position. However, just as mariners of old learned to navigate stormy seas by observing the stars and atmospheric conditions, leaders too can steer their teams through turbulence by adopting adaptive strategies, embodying mindfulness, and fostering resilience.

3.1. Understanding and Accepting Uncertainty

Uncertainty in business arises from numerous sources: economic volatility, technological advances, regulatory changes, societal transformations, and even unexpected global events like pandemics. Instead of resisting uncertainty, leaders must first accept it as an inherent part of the business landscape. This acceptance forms the foundation for all subsequent steps in navigating uncertainty. Once leaders develop the mindset that uncertainty is not an exception but rather a norm, they can devise methods to confront it. This approach allows them to see uncertainty not as a threat, but an opportunity for pioneering changes and growth. Remember, sometimes the densest clouds herald the brightest days.

3.2. Embrace Adaptive Strategies

Adaptive strategies are all about preparing for multiple possible futures rather than trying to predict one precise outcome. Such strategies involve contingency planning and resource reallocation, which enable organizations to respond swiftly and effectively to changing conditions./

Chapter 4. Contingency Planning

Organizations can mitigate uncertainty by developing a variety of contingency plans tailored to potential outcomes. By establishing a range of plausible scenarios — from the most likely to the least likely, from the most optimistic to the most pessimistic — companies can map out in advance how they will react to each possibility.

Chapter 5. Resource Reallocation

Adaptive strategies also call for resource flexibility. Rather than disbursing resources broadly and thinly, a good adaptive strategy may channel resources into specific, targeted investments that align with the organization's strategic goals. This kind of intentional and versatile resource allocation permits companies to pivot whenever necessary.

5.1. Cultivating Mindfulness in Leadership

Mindful leadership involves awareness and acceptance of the present state, leading with compassion, and promoting psychological safety. Four fundamental pillars of mindfulness in leadership are self-awareness, regulation of personal bias, mental agility, and compassion/empathy.

Chapter 6. Self-Awareness

Self-awareness makes a leader sensitive to internal and external cues that could affect decision-making. It helps leaders identify how they react to stressful situations and make conscious efforts to manage these responses effectively.

Chapter 7. Regulation of Personal Bias

Every person carries unconscious biases that can cloud judgment. By recognizing this, leaders can train themselves to question their assumptions and encourage teams to do the same, promoting more objective and unbiased decisions.

Chapter 8. Mental Agility

Mental agility allows leaders to alter their thinking paradigms swiftly, responding efficiently to ever-changing environments. It is about understanding the dynamic nature of situations and integrating different perspectives to drive the most appropriate action.

Chapter 9. Compassion/Empathy

Leaders who display compassion and empathy understand others' perspectives, promoting a more inclusive work environment. This emotional connection bridges the gap between the management and the team, promoting a sense of community and cohesion during uncertainty.

9.1. Fostering Resilience: The Bedrock of Competence in Uncertainty

Resilience is the capacity to recover quickly from difficulties. But, it's not just about bouncing back; it's also about developing toughness and flexibility to handle future unknowns. Key elements of fostering resilience are creating a safety culture, practicing flexibility and adaptability, and focusing on continual learning.

Chapter 10. Creating a Safety Culture

An environment where team members feel physically, emotionally, and psychologically safe is conducive to risk-taking and innovation — a perfect antidote to uncertainty. This safety promotes productive dialogue and empowers individuals to contribute unique, sometimes out-of-the-box solutions.

Chapter 11. Practicing Flexibility and Adaptability

As change becomes the only constant, flexibility and adaptability are critical. Leaders must embrace change as an opportunity to learn, grow, and transform their organization. This adaptive mindset, when modeled by leaders, often permeates throughout the company.

Chapter 12. Continual Learning

Uncertainty is often due to a lack of knowledge. By inculcating a learning culture within the organization, leaders can make their teams better equipped to tackle the unknown. Leaders should emphasize the importance of continuous learning and development, making them fundamental to the organization's strategy.

Navigating uncertainty might be challenging, but with understanding and adaptive strategies, mindfulness, and resilience, leaders of all sectors can steer their organizations toward success. As John C. Maxwell said: "Change is inevitable. Growth is optional." So, let's grow, embracing change and uncertainty as a driving force propelling us towards those stable summits.

Chapter 13. The Art of Decision-Making in Times of Crisis

Decision-making in times of crisis is an art – one that requires leaders to galvanize their cognitive faculties, emotional intelligence, and moral compass to guide their organizations through precarious junctures. Often, the decisions taken during such times can make or break an organization, underscoring the paramount importance of mastering this complex craft.

13.1. Frameworks for Crisis Decision Making

When under pressure, leaders must fall back on proven decision-making frameworks. At the core of such frameworks is a commitment to clarity and consistency. The Cynefin framework, for instance, can help leaders identify the nature of their crisis situation – whether it's simple, complicated, complex, or chaotic – and tailor their decisions accordingly. Another pivotal model is the OODA (Observe, Orient, Decide, Act) loop, which fosters agility in decision-making by emphasizing information gathering, putting the intel into context, drafting decisions, and executing them.

However, while these frameworks can offer cardinal directions, it's the refined judgement of leaders that handle the steering wheel. This is particularly crucial in complex or chaotic scenarios, where there's no room for cookie-cutter solutions and pre-set models may falter.

13.2. Embrace Uncertainty

Uncertainty is an inevitable element of crisis situations, presenting an undulating landscape riddled with blind spots. But rather than stewing in the discomfort, leaders need to bear the banner of resilience. Adopting a positive sum perspective can help reframe ambiguity as a chance to innovate and adapt. Organizational exercises like scenario planning and crisis simulations can also hone the skill of uncertainty navigation, preparing leaders and their teams for various eventualities.

13.3. Information Mastery

In the face of a crisis, sifting through the cacophony of noise to grasp useful information becomes a critical task. Leaders need to develop an interdisciplinary understanding, connecting unfamiliar dots to create an integrated, sensible pattern. Equally important is the skill to disregard information that adds no value. In essence, leaders must seek to convert data to wisdom – a transition that dictates the success rate of crisis navigation.

13.4. Listening to Intuition

While rational, methodical decision-making can steer the ship in normal times, crisis situations may call for the stirrings of intuition. This doesn't indicate hasty, brash decisions, but rather harnessing years of experience and honed instinct to make rapid, yet impactful choices. Leaders must be cautious while exercising this, however, as unchecked biases and assumptions can corrode the objectivity of this decision-making process.

13.5. Ethical Dilemmas: Navigating the Gray

Turbulent times may throw up ethical quandaries, drawing leaders into the dim light of moral ambiguity. Here, they must manage the delicate equilibrium of stakeholder interests, while upholding their own values and those of the organization. Ethical decision-making frameworks, such as the ethics of care, justice, virtue, or utility, may lend some guidance. But ultimately, it's the leader's moral courage that supports these weighty decisions.

13.6. Communication: The Tie that Binds

An adept crisis leader proves themselves not only in making brave decisions but in clearly communicating these choices and underlying reasoning to their team. Transparent, empathetic, and regular communication helps mitigate fear and confusion, building a shared sense of purpose and direction.

13.7. Reflect and Learn

Post-crisis reflection is instrumental in cementing lessons learned, offering an opportunity to dissect decisions made, decipher their impact, and recommend future strategies. Having a systematic approach to learning from past crises can help transform failures into stepping stones for future success.

In a nutshell, the art of decision-making in times of crisis blends science and intuition, courage and caution, personal judgments, and collective wisdom. It's the very fulcrum on which organizational destiny pivots during critical times. By mastering the myriad facets of this art, leaders can not only survive in the menacing face of adversity but thrive by transforming crises into opportunities.

Chapter 14. Mindful Communication: The Key to Fostering Trust

In a world that is persistently replete with uncertainty and change, effective communication is the glue that holds teams and organizations together. It allows leaders to foster trust, build relationships, inspire teams, and navigate the choppy waters of organizational turbulence. To elevate this crucial skill, we assert that the essence of effective communication is mindfulness.

14.1. Mindfulness: A Deeper Dive

Mindfulness is an age-old practice with roots in Eastern traditions, which has been trending in Western societies, thanks to its various health and performance benefits. It is simply the act of being present in the moment, maintaining an open and non-judgmental state of mind. Through the lens of communication, mindfulness refers to a deep awareness and understanding of how one's messages are created, delivered, and perceived.

14.2. The Power of Mindful Communication

Quite often, what leaders believe they communicate doesn't reach the intended recipients precisely as desired, creating gaps, misunderstandings, and, subsequently, trust issues. Mindful communication can bridge these gaps. By being fully present in a conversation, leaders can fully comprehend their messaging, emotional undertones and their team's perspectives, leading to more effective, empathetic communication.

Mindful communication ensures all parties feel heard and understood, fostering an environment of trust and openness. Trust has a domino effect, triggering loyalty, mutual respect, and solid teamwork, which are critical for organizational success, especially during trying times.

14.3. Principles of Mindful Communication

Mindful communication is underpinned by several key principles. Let's explore them below:

1. **Non-judging:** Mindful communicators listen with an open mind, suspending judgments and biases. They value others' viewpoints, even if contradicting with theirs, fostering an environment that encourages open, honest conversation.

2. **Patience:** Instead of rushing to conclusions or actions, mindful leaders patiently carve their communication, ensuring clarity without the urgency.

3. **Beginner's Mind:** Every conversation is a new experience. A "beginner's mind" approach, openness to new possibilities, promotes constructive conversations and learning experiences.

Incorporate these principles in daily communication to instill mindfulness and see vast improvements.

14.4. Tips for Fostering Mindful Communication

Bringing mindfulness to your communication is easier than it might seem. Here are some practical steps:

1. **Active Listening:** Active listening is the key to effective, mindful

communication. Pay undivided attention to what is being said, show empathy and respond thoughtfully.

2. **Practice Silence:** Leaders often feel compelled to fill conversations with words. However, mindful leaders understand the power of silence, offering time for reflection and consciousness, fostering better understanding and trust.

3. **Sanitize your language:** Avoid using any language that may seem aggressive, judgmental, or inflammatory.

4. **Mindful Responses:** Respond to conversations, conflicts, or challenges with composure and thoughtfulness. Crises often demand quick responses, but a mindful response – measured and reflective – is usually the most effective.

5. **Practicing Mindfulness:** The path to becoming a mindful communicator starts with practicing mindfulness in everyday life. Activities like meditation, yoga, and establishing moments of silence throughout your day can help instill a mindful lifestyle.

14.5. Case Study: A Corporate Leader's Triumph with Mindful Communication

As a defining trait, Amy, the CEO of a multinational corporation, applied mindful communication as a crisis management tool during the most stormy period of her leadership. When the sustainability of her organization was under threat due to macroeconomic factors, Amy tailored her messages with care and mindfulness. Her communication, transparent and honest, yet empathetic and understanding of the challenges faced by her employees, instilled a sense of trust and unity within the organization.

Through mindful listening, she stayed in tune with her employees, understanding their deepest concerns, fears and suggestions, further solidifying their trust in her leadership. Her calm demeanor in the face of the storm encouraged her employees in doing their share of the heavy lifting, resulting in the company emerging from the crisis stronger and triumphant.

Amy's success story underscores the significant role that mindful communication plays in fostering trust and navigating turbulent times. By understanding the principles, practicing the tips, and learning from real-world examples, leaders can enhance their mindful communication skills to foster trust and stability within their organizations.

Emphasize on mindful communication to promote understanding, building communities steeped in trust and respect, reinforcing the ability to weather any storm. After all, stability doesn't occur in the absence of storms but in understanding how to steer the ship amidst them. Mindful communication equips leaders with this mastery.

Chapter 15. The Power of Adaptability: Embracing Change and Innovation

The modern leader is confronted with an intimidating reality: the only constant in today's world is continuous, relentless change. Change's chameleon-like nature means it is often unpredictable, sometimes beneficial, and other times, not so much. It is this uncertain nature of change that can undermine even the most robust organisations, causing disarray and reducing efficiency. This chapter aims to illuminate the comprehensive powers of adaptability, demonstrating how to positively embrace change and innovation, and thus, navigate through the unpredictable waters of organisational leadership.

15.1. Adaptability: A Critical Leadership Skill

Adaptability is the capacity to modify or adjust one's behaviors, tasks, and mindsets in response to new information, changing circumstances, or unexpected obstacles. It turns traditional leaders—static in their approach, resistant to deviation—into dynamic pillars of adaptability.

A study conducted by the Center for Creative Leadership found that executives who are adaptable are more likely to succeed. Those who showed an aptitude for adaptability were able to work more effectively in international assignments, navigate through complex business situations, and handle high levels of uncertainty with ease.

15.2. Embracing Change: An Evolutionary Necessity

Research from the field of evolutionary biology provides a vivid illustration of the critical importance of adaptability. Species that are able to adjust their behavior and strategy to respond to changing environments survive, while those that can't, face extinction. This principle holds true in the business world; organisations that embrace change proactively possess a distinct advantage over those that are reactive or resist change.

Negotiating change requires visionary leadership. Leaders who can anticipate and plan for change, communicative transparently, and shift their strategy when required, lead their teams efficaciously through periods of disruption.

15.3. Innovation: The Lifeline in Turbulent Times

Innovation is often perceived as a jargon-packed code word for "new ideas". However, it's more than just introducing a groundbreaking product or service. It encapsulates an entire ecosystem of attitudes, actions, and behaviors contributing towards an environment that rewards thinking differently.

Leaders who prioritize innovation often utilize techniques such as encouraging creative thought, challenging existing norms, and fostering a culture of continuous learning. The benefits are twofold—on one hand, they engender a high-performing, involved workforce; on the other, they are better positioned to handle market shifts and customer demands.

15.4. Creating an Agile Organization

Building an organisation that is essentially adaptable and innovative involves establishing an agile framework. Agile organizations have structural and cultural components that allow them to react quickly to change. Their leaders value experimentation, learning, and quick decisions. They flatten hierarchies allowing for faster communication, and they encourage a sense of ownership among their employees.

In a volatile world, agility becomes a key component for sustainability. The leaders of agile organizations understand that change and uncertainty are not only inevitable, but also significant opportunities to learn, grow, and innovate.

15.5. Conclusion: The Power of Adaptability

Without question, adaptability is a vital leadership capability—one that requires understanding, embracing and leveraging change, and fostering an innovation culture within your organization. It is a challenging yet rewarding journey and seizing its manifold benefits can usher in a new era of success in these turbulent times.

The challenges that change and uncertainty pose are daunting, but the opportunities are exhilarating. So, as you navigate your leadership journey, stay flexible, stay adaptable, and above all, stay open to the transformative power of change and innovation.

Chapter 16. Leading with Empathy: The Value of Emotional Intelligence

In the realm of effective leadership, emotional intelligence and empathy play pivotal roles. More than canned strategies or company processes, understanding and addressing human emotions can serve as the lighthouse guiding a leader's decisions, often steering an organization successfully through turbulent times.

16.1. Building an Understanding of Emotional Intelligence

Emotional Intelligence (EI), as defined by psychologists John D. Mayer and Peter Salovey, is the ability to recognize, understand, and control our own emotions, as well as the ability to recognize, understand, and influence the emotions of others. In short, it gives us the tools to ascertain and manage what's happening beneath the surface, both within ourselves and others.

For leaders, EI is not only highly desirable but also crucial. It fuels those micro decisions that breathe life into an empathetic management style — understanding employees' feelings, channeling their motivation, and soothing their anxieties. So, how can we nurture this vital leadership quality?

1. **Self-awareness**: This is about understanding your emotions and their impact on others. This involves self-reflection, where a leader analyzes their reactions and responses to different situations.

2. **Self-management**: Here, a leader exercises control over their emotions, preventing negative feelings from affecting their

decision-making or interactions.

3. **Social awareness**: In this aspect, leaders tap into their empathy, becoming adept at understanding their team members' feelings while staying attuned to the dynamics between team members.

4. **Relationship management**: Leaders nurture their relationships employing understanding and effective interactions. This includes conflict resolution, influence, inspiration, and more.

16.2. Embracing Empathy: The Heart of Leadership

Empathy, a core component of EI, deepens the connection between leaders and their team. Empathetic leadership isn't about feeling others' emotions but rather understanding them, stepping into their shoes to grasp their point of view. It allows leaders to nurture genuine relationships, paving a trustworthy path filled with open communication and mutual understanding.

There are three kinds of empathy that every leader should embody:

1. **Cognitive Empathy**: Involves understanding others' perspectives or thought processes, enabling better communication and problem-solving.

2. **Emotional Empathy**: Feeling what others are feeling, enabling us to share experiences at an emotional level deepening interpersonal connections.

3. **Compassionate Empathy**: More than understanding or feeling, this type of empathy spurs action, driving us to help alleviate others' suffering.

16.3. The Empathy-Performance Connection

Empathetic leaders foster work environments where team members feel valued and understood — leading to increased engagement, productivity, and loyalty. Studies (such as "The Business Case for Emotional Intelligence," Consortium for Research on Emotional Intelligence in Organizations, 2010) have also linked managers' emotional intelligence with team performance and employee job satisfaction.

Consider Google's Project Aristotle, which sought to uncover the secret behind effective teams. Surprisingly, it wasn't about who was on the team but how the team worked together. The study found that 'psychological safety', a factor that requires strong EI from leaders, was the most crucial aspect of high-performing teams.

Further research also suggests that empathy leads to stronger customer relationships, encouraging customer loyalty and positive brand reputation.

16.4. Strengthening EI and Empathy: A Practical Guide

Leaders can develop both EI and empathy through deliberate practices:

1. **Practice active listening**: Seek to understand before being understood. Listen without interrupting and validate the speaker's emotions.

2. **Invite feedback**: Create a feedback-friendly environment to understand others' perspectives about you and the situation.

3. **Embrace different perspectives**: Promote a culture where

differing viewpoints are welcomed.

4. **Mindfulness**: Practice being present, it helps attune to your emotional state and the feelings of others.

5. **Lead by example**: Show empathy in your actions. This includes understanding, respecting, and accommodating different work styles.

Indeed, leading with empathy and EI provides the bedrock for strong relationships and highly functional teams. By embracing these qualities, leaders can navigate uncertain times, bolster team spirit, and create working environments where everyone feels valued and heard.

In essence, emotional intelligence and empathy aren't just 'nice-to-have' leadership traits; they are essential ingredients for successful leadership and team performance, particularly in volatile, changing business landscapes. No longer locked in academia, these concepts need to be operationalized, serving as guiding principles that shape our leadership style, allowing us to scale the highest summits with our teams, even amidst turbulent times. After all, everyone would agree that the voyage becomes smoother when the captain truly understands the crew.

Chapter 17. Steadfast Vision: Preserving Organization's Goals in Uncertain Times

In an era marked by rapid technological advances, economic shocks, political volatility, and a global pandemic, the only certainty for all organizations is uncertainty. Yet, it is in these tumultuous times that organizations need to stay resolute in their mission and tenaciously focused on their long-term goals. Commitment to a steadfast vision matters more now than ever.

17.1. Into The Fog

The moment crises hit us, the first natural human response is fear. It's easy to get lost, disoriented, and even panic-stricken in this fog of fear and uncertainty. Uncertainty arouses apprehension, and such a negative emotional state can easily pervade the organization, causing disarrangement and chaos. It is here that we begin to understand why a tenacious focus on our goals is crucial.

Preserving an organization's goals provides a beacon that pierces through this dense fog. It gives the organization and its team a familiar point of orientation to navigate towards - a constant, unperturbed by the swirling turmoil that surrounds it. Like mariners in uncharted waters charting their course by the steadfast North Star, organizations can leverage their core goals as fixed points of reference.

17.2. The Power of a Steadfast Vision

A steadfast vision brings continuity, as it serves as the compass that consistently directs every member of your team. It offers stability, fostering trust and confidence amidst a sea of change. It is the thread that holds together the patchwork of an organization's initiatives, weaving them into a coherent whole whose sum is greater than its parts.

Yet, possessing a steadfast vision goes beyond merely having a few neatly-worded values or mission statements on company brochures or website. It requires deliberate actions to infuse this vision into the everyday work experienced by every team member. It requires consistency so that it can act as a touchstone during times of uncertainty.

To achieve this, the leaders must clearly articulate the organization's vision, crystallize it into actionable goals, and form a strategic plan that allows the team to keep sight of these goals even amidst turbulent waters. The leaders need to stir a sense of unity, cohesion, and purpose through frequently communicating the vision, and evidently aligning their actions to it.

17.3. Sailing through the Storm

When a storm hits, it is not the time to question the destination. It is the time to adjust the sails and reassess the path we are taking to reach it. Dealing with immediate crises and maintain a steadfast focus on long-term goals is a delicate balancing act for leaders.

In dire situations, leaders can easily lose sight of long-term goals, becoming solely reactive responding to each incoming wave of emergencies and crises. This short-termism trap is dangerous, as it could lead to misallocation of resources, missed opportunities, and eventually, loss of direction.

Avoid this pitfall by creating an adaptive navigation plan. This plan should make provisions for potential crises and uncertainties, therefore enabling your organization to react swiftly and efficiently when surprises arrive. It includes adaptive mechanisms enabling the organization to adjust its tactical maneuvers without losing sight of its strategic objectives.

Remember, leaders' emphasis should be on steering the ship rather than stopping the storm. Those who act proactively, adapt swiftly, but don't lose track of their vision, fare the best.

17.4. Leadership in Practice: Case Studies

Consider the case of Airbnb. When "stay-at-home" orders swept across the globe in 2020, the travel industry collapsed. Despite this unprecedented crisis, Airbnb's leadership didn't lose sight of their long-term vision: "Creating a world where anyone can belong anywhere." They quickly adapted by launching 'Online Experiences' and providing remote stays, thus demonstrating how a steadfast focus on the vision can lead organizations through.

Similarly, Microsoft during the 2008 economic downturn remained committed to their vision of innovating technology to empower businesses and people globally. They increased R&D spending, leading to the development of Cloud Computing - a game-changing leap that catapulted them ahead of their competitors when the economic condition revived.

17.5. Establishing your Steadfast Vision

It begins with introspection and clearly articulating your vision. Creating a vision isn't about predicting the future; it's about making a thoughtful decision on what we want it to be and committing to it. Once you've established your vision, communicate it repeatedly and clearly within the organization. Be the exemplar by aligning your actions with the expressed vision.

Use your vision as the touchstone for decision-making, thereby building consistency. Include it in your strategic planning, creating a roadmap that weaves your vision into every facet of the organization. Establish robust feedback loops, so you can monitor how your team is interpreting and contributing to the vision. Celebrate the successes along the way, and enable and empower every team member to contribute to this collective vision.

To sum up, a steadfast vision is the guiding compass through the fog of uncertainty and turmoil. It's not about resisting the storm, but learning how to sail in it and continuing onward towards your destination. With a clearly articulated and well-communicated vision, every decision, every strategy, and every action become parts of a unified journey, leading your organization always forward - towards the summit that you've envisioned!

Chapter 18. Cultivating Team Resilience: Building a Supportive Environment

The environment a team operates in molds their ability to withstand trials and tribulations. A key leadership task, therefore, is nurturing a supportive environment that promotes resilience. This results not only in heightened productivity but also abundant creativity and innovation. This chapter will delve into the various strategies leaders can employ to foster a supportive and resilient team culture.

18.1. Emphasising Psychological Safety

Creating a psychologically secure environment allows team members to voice their thoughts and queries without fear. This entails establishing a culture of respect and authenticity where everyone feels valued. To achieve this, leaders should regularly engage team members in open conversations, promoting transparency. Devoting time to listening cultivates trust and robust relationships.

When psychological safety is upheld, it paves the way for candid discussions about mistakes. Accepting that errors are an integral part of learning encourages a growth mindset: challenges are perceived as opportunities to better oneself, and failures as stepping stones to success.

An excellent way to action this is by carrying out blameless post-mortems after project completions. Here, the emphasis isn't on fault-finding but on joint understanding of what went astray and how to rectify it. Leaders need to steer these sessions with finesse, ensuring a positive outcome.

18.2. Encouraging Emotional Intelligence

Emotional intelligence, the capacity to comprehend and manage emotions, plays a crucial role in building team resilience, fostering empathy and understanding among colleagues. A leader with high emotional intelligence is proficient in recognizing their team members' emotions and responding appropriately.

You stimulate emotional intelligence within your team by endorsing effective communication. Host workshops and training sessions that help your team identify, express, and manage their emotions better. An emotionally intelligent team is not just aware of each other's feelings but also empathetic to the emotional weather of their colleagues.

18.3. Promoting Work-Life Balance

Striving for an equitable balance between professional obligations and personal life boosts morale and job satisfaction. Establish policies that honor this balance. Flexible work schedules, remote working options, and providing ample paid time-off can help.

Maintaining an emphasis on performance outcomes rather than time spent at work can be beneficial. A results-oriented work environment (ROWE) ensures that employees are evaluated on their performance and productivity, not their working hours.

18.4. Cultivating Open Communication

Seamless communication is a cornerstone of a supportive working environment. Encourage discussions and feedback, both top-down and bottom-up. This can be achieved by:

- Hosting regular team meetings: Provide an open platform for everyone to discuss their ideas and concerns.
- Encouraging feedback culture: Constructive feedback paves the way for continuous improvement.
- Utilizing multiple channels of communication: This can range from in-person meetings to emails and enterprise social networking platforms.

18.5. Encouraging Peer Support

Crucial for team resilience is a supportive network among peers. Foster an environment where colleagues see themselves as allies rather than competitors. Team building events and informal social gatherings can help members bond and form stronger relationships.

18.6. Training for Resilience

Resilience can be honed through specific training programs designed to instill coping mechanisms in individuals. Such initiatives can range from mindfulness-based stress reduction (MBSR) to cognitive behavioral skills training. Offering these resources presents employees with tools to manage stress and prevent burnout.

18.7. Building a Diverse Team

Inclusivity breeds resilience. A diverse team allows for a multitude of perspectives and solutions to challenges, inevitably improving adaptability. Celebrate differences, value everyone's contribution, and promote an environment of mutual respect and understanding.

In conclusion, fostering a resilient team isn't a one-time effort but a continuous process. Aim for steady improvements over time.

Genuine and purposeful efforts to create a supportive atmosphere will not go unnoticed by your team, and will pay dividends in their resilience, productivity, and overall performance.

Chapter 19. Sustaining Momentum: Ensuring Performance Amidst Disruptions

In the journey of leadership, maintaining momentum amidst the tumult of change and disruption is key - it's the equivalent of keeping the sails straight in stormy seas. While it demands agility, adaptability, and resilience, careful strategy and mindful reactions can guide you towards this goal. Let's journey through the fundamentals of maintaining momentum, braiding theory with real-world scenarios to produce a deep, practical understanding.

19.1. Navigating Through Uncertainty

As leaders, disruptive times can seem frighteningly vast and opaque—like an unchartable ocean. However, it's pertinent to perceive them as opportunities for growth and innovation. Embrace uncertainty with an open, adaptive mindset, rather than avoiding it.

Risk-taking is an inherent and essential part of leadership. Stepping into unchartered territories might seem daunting, but bear in mind that every innovation history applauds commenced as risks. The key lies in infusing risk-taking with astute judgment, a deep understanding of all stakeholders involved, and an unwavering commitment to your organization's mission and values.

19.2. Building a Resilient Team

A pivotal factor in sustaining momentum is building an adaptable and resilient team. A sturdy ship is paramount to surviving the storm, and your team is your ship. Here, focus on creating a culture that expects change and is ready to adapt when it arrives.

Facilitating open communication is quintessential to this process. Make sure every member feels heard and appreciated. Empower them to voice their ideas, concerns, and struggles. This encourages a sense of mutual respect and shared responsibility, in turn, strengthening your team.

Boosting your team's resilience also necessitates training and development programs that enhance their skills and capacity to cope with changes. Done right, these initiatives will equip your team with the proper tools to handle unforeseen challenges effectively.

19.3. Cultivating Adaptability

Embrace change. Adaptability is the elixir that can turn all disruptions beneficial. It's not about perfecting a static plan but having the ability to pivot your strategies in response to unexpected situations.

Before you adapt, however, discern between necessary and unnecessary changes. The discernment comes from a deep understanding of your organization's mission statement, culture, and long-term goals. Once identified, communicate the necessary changes to your team, emphasizing the reasons and benefits associated with them.

19.4. Fostering Innovation

Innovation is the beacon that can lead organizations out of the tumultuous waters of change and disruption. It is conjured through open-mindedness, creativity, and an ecosphere where failures are seen as fertile grounds for learning, rather than dire mistakes.

One tangible way to infuse innovation in your organization is by providing time, space, and resources for brainstorming and experimentation. Encouraging cross-departmental interactions can also lead to diverse perspectives, potentially sparking creative ideas.

19.5. Measuring Success Amidst Change

In a changing landscape, success cannot be measured by past benchmarks. Instead, consider creating new measures that align with your current circumstances and long-term goals. It could be related to how effectively your team adapts to changes, the number of innovative ideas implemented, or the extent of positive customer feedback amid crises.

19.6. Engaging and Communicating With Stakeholders

In the course of disruptions, engage with your stakeholders - employees, customers, investors, communities, and keep them in the loop. Clear, consistent communication eases tension, builds relationship, and enhances trust—further stabilizing your foothold amidst rough times.

Stakeholder communication should be authentic, empathetic, and transparent. Acknowledge the situation, discuss its impacts, and lay out the actions you're taking. Offering regular updates showcases your preparedness and commitment, reinforcing your image as a reliable, resilient leader.

19.7. Implementing Focus and Flexibility

Successful leaders not only stay focused on their mission but can also flex and adapt their strategies to circumvent challenges. The sweet spot is to be flexible without losing sight of your core goals.

Train your gaze on the bigger picture, ensuring disruptions don't obscure your vision. Simultaneously, stay cognizant of ground realities and be ready to modify your approaches while staying aligned to your ultimate goal.

Navigating the stormy seas of business disruptions can be an arduous task, but with the right mindset, strategies and approaches, it's possible to sustain momentum. Remember, disruptions need not derail; instead, they can pave the way for new paths and opportunities. It's in your hands (or at your helm), how you navigate them. Stay adaptable, stay resilient, and sail on towards stable summits.

Chapter 20. Balancing Act: Maintaining Work-Life Harmony in Pressing Times

In today's rapidly changing and often uncertain world, the line between work and personal life becomes increasingly blurred. The integration of technology into our daily lives, coupled with the recent global shift towards remote work due to the COVID-19 pandemic, means that it is now more important than ever to maintain a healthy work-life balance.

Balancing work commitments and personal life is a delicate act - like juggling, where one's attention is constantly shifting and where a single slip can bring the whole act down. But handle this balancing act well, and you'll find that it becomes easier to manage the pressures of leading during turbulent times.

20.1. The Era of Permeable Boundaries

Working from home, once a luxury, has become the norm for millions of workers worldwide. The same devices we use for work are often those we use for personal activities, from sending emails and attending virtual meetings to scrolling social media or watching Netflix. What once were distinct realms of work and home have meshed into one, leading to a feeling of perpetual 'on-call' status. Notions of regular working hours have blurred, and the boundary between professional and personal life is becoming more permeable.

Adding to this mix is the inherent pressure that comes with leadership. The responsibility of decision-making, managing teams, responding to crises and steering the organization can add up, often resulting in leaders working around the clock. To address these challenges, finding ways to delineate and balance personal and professional time is essential.

20.2. Mindfulness: A Key to Balance

At its core, maintaining work-life harmony is about mindfulness. When we are present in the moment, we can acknowledge when we are tipping towards work or personal life and take corrective action.

However, mindfulness goes beyond just being present. It involves understanding the impact of our actions, emotions, and decisions, both on our well-being and that of others. Are you so engrossed in your work that your family life suffers? Or is your dedication to your job causing you to neglect your physical health?

Taking the time to examine our situation with a mindful eye can provide invaluable insights into how we can bring about balance. Moreover, applying mindfulness strategies such as focused breathing, meditation, or yoga can help ensure work-related stress doesn't bleed into our personal lives.

20.3. Creating a Work-Life Harmony Blueprint

A practical step in achieving work-life harmony is crafting a 'blueprint'. This personalized guide should specify your priorities, boundaries, and strategies to achieve balance in your life.

1. Prioritize: Start by identifying what is most important to you in both your professional and personal life. This can serve as a guiding light when making decisions that affect your work-life balance.

2. Set Boundaries: Define clear demarcations between work and

personal life, whether that's setting specific working hours, having a separate work and home workspace, or scheduling dedicated 'digital detox' periods.

3. Balance Strategies: Implement strategies to balance work pressures with personal life. This could be dedicating time for physical activities, adopting mindfulness practices, or simply taking time to disconnect from work.

20.4. Flexibility and Understanding: Essential Leadership Traits

As a leader, it is not only important to find our balance, but to also promote the same among our team members. Leaders should create an environment that encourages a healthy work-life balance, showing empathy by understanding the unique pressures team members face.

To foster a healthy balance for your team, consider adopting flexible working hours, having regular check-ins to gauge pressure levels, providing resources for stress management, and actively promoting taking time off. Empowering your team to establish their work-life harmony can lead to improved productivity, enhanced job satisfaction, and a more positive work atmosphere.

20.5. A Culture of Balance

Shifting organizational culture to support work-life harmony can alleviate the pressure and stress felt both by leaders and their teams. Leaders play a key role in initiating and implementing this cultural shift by modeling the balance they wish to see, openly discussing the importance of work-life harmony, and setting policies that facilitate balance.

Incorporating work-life balance into the organization's culture may involve implementing a flexible work schedule policy, providing resources for mental health and stress management, or plainly encouraging employees to take time for themselves and their families.

20.6. Conclusion: The Balancing Act is Ongoing

Maintaining a healthy work-life balance isn't a one-time goal. It requires continuous effort, reevaluation, and adaptation to new circumstances. The act of balancing will fluctuate as pressures change - sometimes swaying towards work or personal life.

Yet, the key lies in recognizing these shifts in balance and taking proactive steps to level out once more. It involves prioritizing mental well-being, setting healthy boundaries, and promoting a culture of work-life harmony both for yourself and within your organization. The ongoing balancing act is not one to be dreaded, but rather embraced as a sign of our capability to adapt, thrive, and lead amidst life's constant changes.